DUST AND LIGHT

DUST AND LIGHT

BY

JOHN HALL WHEELOCK

AUTHOR OF

"THE HUMAN FANTASY," "THE BELOVED ADVENTURE,"
"LOVE AND LIBERATION"

> —they are still immortal
> Who, through birth's orient portal
> And death's dark chasm hurrying to and fro,
> Clothe their unceasing flight
> In the brief dust and light
> Gathered around their chariots as they go—
>
> —SHELLEY.

NEW YORK
CHARLES SCRIBNER'S SONS
1921

TO

HARRIET ANNE WEINERT

IN GRATITUDE FOR HER HELP
IN THE PREPARATION OF THESE PAGES
FOR THE PRESS

Thanks are due to the editors of *Scribner's Magazine*, *The Century*, *Harper's Monthly*, *The American Magazine*, *The Forum*, *The Smart Set*, *The Bellman*, *The Bookman*, *The Dial*, *Poetry*, *The International*, *The Poetry Journal*, *Reedy's Mirror*, *McClure's Magazine*, *Contemporary Verse*, *The Lyric*, *The Poetry Review*, *Youth*, *The Art World*, *The Yale Review*, etc., for their courteous permission to reprint many of the following poems.

CONTENTS

CONTENTS

CONTENTS

CONTENTS

I

GLIMMERING EARTH

Now fade the conflicts and the clamourings
Of the loud day ; a steadier hand and higher
Across the broad bosom of Creation's strings
Draws the most holy bow of deep desire.

CLOUDLESS MOONRISE

BRANCHES, drenched with dew,
 Through the moonlight loom,
Drifted moonlight lies
 Deep across the room.

Through the glimmering aisles
 And wild country ways
Drifts the fragrant mist,
 Like a cloud that strays.

Far, and far around
 The grasshoppers' shrill
Shimmers, and a lone
 Cricket from the hill

Cries "I love, I love."
 Heaven's holy bound
Overflows with calm
 Radiance all around.

Heaven is like a room
 Bared, immense and bright.

CLOUDLESS MOONRISE

Earth, each bush and tree,
 Drinks the solemn light.

On her parted lips,
 Lost in slumber, lies
The unuttered word
 Out of Paradise.

EARTH

GRASSHOPPER, your fairy song
    And my poem alike belong
To the dark and silent earth
From which all poetry has birth;
All we say and all we sing
Is but as the murmuring
Of that drowsy heart of hers
When from her deep dream she stirs:
If we sorrow, or rejoice,
You and I are but her voice.

Deftly does the dust express
In mind her hidden loveliness,
And from her cool silence stream
The cricket's cry and Dante's dream;
For the earth that breeds the trees
Breeds cities too, and symphonies.
Equally her beauty flows
Into a savior, or a rose—
Looks down in dream, and from above
Smiles at herself in Jesus' love.
Christ's love and Homer's art

EARTH

Are but the workings of her heart;
Through Leonardo's hand she seeks
Herself, and through Beethoven speaks
In holy thunderings around
The awful message of the ground.

The serene and humble mold
Does in herself all selves enfold—
Kingdoms, destinies, and creeds,
Great dreams, and dauntless deeds,
Science that metes the firmament,
The high, inflexible intent
Of one for many sacrificed—
Plato's brain, the heart of Christ;
All love, all legend, and all lore
Are in the dust forevermore.

Even as the growing grass
Up from the soil religions pass,
And the field that bears the rye
Bears parables and prophecy.
Out of the earth the poem grows
Like the lily, or the rose;
And all man is, or yet may be,
Is but herself in agony

EARTH

Toiling up the steep ascent
Toward the complete accomplishment
When all dust shall be, the whole
Universe, one conscious soul.

Yea, the quiet and cool sod
Bears in her breast the dream of God.

If you would know what earth is, scan
The intricate, proud heart of man,
Which is the earth articulate,
And learn how holy and how great,
How limitless and how profound
Is the nature of the ground—
How without terror or demur
We may entrust ourselves to her
When we are wearied out, and lay
Our faces in the common clay.

For she is pity, she is love,
All wisdom, she, all thoughts that move
About her everlasting breast
Till she gathers them to rest:
All tenderness of all the ages,
Seraphic secrets of the sages,

7

EARTH

Vision and hope of all the seers,
All prayer, all anguish, and all tears
Are but the dust, that from her dream
Awakes, and knows herself supreme—
Are but earth, when she reveals
All that her secret heart conceals
Down in the dark and silent loam,
Which is ourselves, asleep, at home.

Yea, and this, my poem, too,
Is part of her as dust and dew,
Wherein herself she doth declare
Through my lips, and say her prayer.

SEPTEMBER BY THE SEA

THE morning makes a light upon the sea,
    Curving before me, like a crescent moon,
With slender violet waves that gradually
    Kindle into the fiery fields of noon.

Line upon line, out to the farthest rim
    They reach immeasurably, pale as the breast
Of a sick child, and tremulous and dim,
    Save where the wind has kissed them out of rest

So hard it leaves a mark all foam and white.
    O delicate, violet, autumnal sea,
Like a wide field made for the sheer delight
    Of the cold wind to walk on, and be free,

Like a clear harp made for the eager hands
    Of the September wind, chilly and pale!
There is a wistfulness about the lands
    When summer ebbs and all the flowers fail.

Therefore I come to you that guard and keep,
    O changeless one, the memories of all things,

SEPTEMBER BY THE SEA

The dreams of all the world in the vast sleep
    Of the pale waters, drowsy with murmurings.

Here deep Eternity has conquered Time,
    No trace of ruthless autumn lingers here;
But on the shore the roses cease to climb,
    And fading wings ebb with the tidal year.

Love leaves the body, as summer leaves the lands,
    But the waves, like the heart, remembering moan;
Therefore I sit beside you on the sands
    That I may mix my memories with your own:

And the wide, level fields of the flat sea,
    Always the same, reach to the farthest bound,
With waves lifting and lapsing wearily—
    And the eternal heavens all around.

THE LONELY POET

NOW, while the loom of evening spins
    Her veil, the parable begins,
And God with weariless delight
Repeats anew the poem of night.

Softly, softly flows along
The rhythm of the eternal song—
In tremor of light and shade is heard
The lonely Poet's laboring word.

Against the music of the shrill
Grasshopper, and the starry trill
Of the cicadas' cry, the lone
Cricket's harp makes drowsy drone.

And one pale star upon the breast
Of lingering twilight in the west
Trembles, far over in profound
Rapture of light the stars are drowned.

The cup of beauty to the brim
Is filled with cloudy song and dim

11

THE LONELY POET

Shadow of moonlight, everywhere
From earth to heaven ascends the prayer.

O Master, is it not enough!
But no, the insatiate heart of Love,
The Poet's heart, for sheer excess
Heaps loveliness on loveliness.

Hark—from the leafy hill near by
The owlet wakes, and pours his cry
Into the poem of night!   Now grows
Beauty too great.   Heaven overflows.

STORM AND SUN

O LOVE, now the herded billows over the holy plain
 Of the trampled sea move thunderously, and cast
Their wrath on the dark shore—let us set out again,
 Let us make seaward, and be gone at last

Into the choiring, clashing, wild waste of waters strown
 Around us,—forward—forward—, and leave behind
The little frets and the fevers, just we two alone,
 Heart-free, as once in days long out of mind!

Forget the city and all its troubles, leave forever
 Our dusty ways! The Eternal 'round us rolled
Shall wash us white of the little sins and fears that sever,
 Lave us, and leave us lovers as of old—

Lovers as once in golden days gone by, till sorrow
 Fall from us like a robe, the martyrdom
Of life on the daily rack: there shall be no Tomorrow,
 Nor Yesterday, but heaven and ocean.—Sweetheart,
  come

STORM AND SUN

And on the swelling pillow of the Unbounded lean
    Your cheek, all fiery now—O let us press
Forward, the changeful furrows of the flashing foam be-
      tween,
    Our glowing bodies into the Loveliness!

The waves shatter, the billows break us, the sullen wrath
    Of the surf beats down our foreheads. Line on line
Rises the majesty of the sea to oppose our path
    With tingling bodies through the stinging brine;

But in our jubilant breasts the embattled life at bay
    Exults fiercely for joy, the waves cry out
And shout in answering joy, the salt and savage spray
    Showers our shoulders in the exuberant bout,

Where we press forward, laughing for lusty love, and the
      hollows
    Receive us and rise, the foam of the breaker's crest
Unfolds like a flower and dies of its kiss, and subsides, and
      follows,
    Laughing and loving, where our limbs have pressed:

Till in the lustrous shadow of the last wave before us
    We bow, and from the rolling billow's might

STORM AND SUN

Lift glimmering eyelids up, while hearts and lips in chorus
    Mingle with winds and waters their delight.

Far—far—where the sea-bird sinks weary wings at last
    Before the wrath of the wings of the wind, the sea
Makes moan, the inconsolable, pale waters are aghast,
    And shudder with dread of their own immensity.

They murmur with one another, the voice of their vast
        prayer
    Sinks down in supplication, and the sleep
Of the Supreme is stirred to whispers everywhere—
    The dark and divine sorrows of the Deep.

Where the heads of the sea were holy and lifted in wrath
        divine
    Now broods the silence, heaven holds its breath,—
Where the feet of the winds made music far out to the lone
        sea-line,—
    The rapture and awe and silence as of death!

Hark—how the lonely sea-bird screams above the surges
    And inland reaches! Now, far out, we roam
The desert and dumb vast of the dread sea that urges
    Our fitful course far out beyond the foam,

STORM AND SUN

Toward the most pallid rim of cloudy noonday steering
    Steadily, while the fluent glooms and grave
Lap us and lift, repulse, and pause—the wild and veering
    Will of the loving and reluctant wave.

The sombre and immense breast of the huge sea
    Lifts in long lines of beauty, the supreme
Bosom with its vast love rises resistlessly,
    And lapses in long lines into its dream.

Lone to the last marge—lone—lone—lone—
    And void to where the huddled waters crowd
The brim—along the floor of heaven's darkened throne
    Moves, like a ghost, the shadow of a cloud.

Shadow and light pass over shifting, shine and shade
    Vanish and veer, upon the chilly rim
Kindle like crowns the cloud-crests along the east arrayed
    And swords of flame, like swords of the seraphim.

The floors of the sea catch fire, the eye of the world's light
    Dilates, and into a glory of glittering gold
Break the pale greens and purples; the sun in heaven's height
    Unveils himself for all men to behold

And all the world is a-riot, behind us and before,
    With fire and color—the heavens roll back their gloom,

16

STORM AND SUN

From zone to zone, from the zenith to the everlasting floor,
    Reaches one resonant and radiant room—

Light!—Light! The astounded, far fields of ocean shine
    Sheer gold and shimmering amber: where we take
The lips of the wave with laughter your eyes are turned to
    mine,
    Sweetheart, your eyes that burn for beauty's sake.

They tremble with happy tears and little words unspoken
    Trouble your lips; dumbly, dumbly we know
Something starry and strange, that the world's wheel has
    broken,
    Come back to us out of the long-ago.

Put out your hand. O cleave the clasp of the close wave,
    turning
    Its fire to flowers! Put out your hand, and move
Forward into the radiant far reaches 'round us burning,
    Darling, as once in the old days of love.

Our hearts drink the wrath and the wonder, the breath of
    the boundless spaces
    Hallows our foreheads, the exceeding might
Of moving waters around us is music, and on our faces
    The glory of God is shed, His holy light!

17

THANKS FROM EARTH TO HEAVEN

GOD pours for me His draught divine,—
Moonlight, which is the poet's wine,
He has made this perfect night
For my wonder and delight.

What is it He would declare
In this beauty everywhere—
What dearest thought of His is heard
In the moonlight's secret word?

To the human, the Supreme
Poet speaks in wind and stream,
Tenderly He does express
His meaning in each loveliness.

Simply does He speak and clear,
As man to man, His message dear—
Aye—and well enough He knows
Who shall understand His rose!

THANKS FROM EARTH TO HEAVEN

Night is but His parable
Secretly where He would tell,
As to an intimate of His,
The mystery of all that is;

Nor humblest, nor most exquisite
Detail or phrase does He omit
From His great poem, confident
It shall be noted what He meant.

And cunningly doth still devise
New Aprils for His poet's eyes
For whose joy all things were wrought,
That without him were as nought.

Holy Poet, I have heard
Thy lost music, Thy least word;
Not Thy beauty's tiniest part
Has escaped this loving heart!

While the great world goes its way
I watch in wonder all the day,
All the night my spirit sings
For the loveliness of things.

But for lonely men like me
It were wasted utterly
All this beauty, vainly spent,—
Unavailing lavishment.

Little cricket, never fear,
There is one who waits to hear—
Nor is there loveliness so shy
It shall escape a poet's eye.

For the world enough it were
To have a useful earth and bare,
But for poets it is made
All in loveliness arrayed.

For his eye the little moth
Wears her coat of colored cloth,
And to please his ear the deep
Ocean murmurs in her sleep.

Rustle gently in the breeze
For his delight the poplar trees,
And in the song within his head
The thanks from earth to heaven is said.

MIDNIGHT

Now in the still
    Shadow and glamour of the departed sun
Beauty's immortal ritual is done,
    The divine word and will.

    Now, lost in lone
Worship and breathless adoration, lies
The loving at the belovèd breast and cries
    His prayer up to her throne.

    Now thrills the dim
Heart of compassionate and conquering love
With solemn pride, and from her throne above
    Listens, and leans to him.

    No sound is here.
Mysteriously the many are made one.—
O peace, now the eternal will is done,
    And God's own heart how near!

THE MOONLIGHT SONATA

GLIMMERING meadows miles around,
Drenched with dew and drowsy sound,
Drink the moonlight and the dream.
Veiled in mists the lowlands seem,
Through wild ways and fragrant aisles
Of the country, miles on miles,
Drifting cloudlike without will,
And soft mist is on the hill.

Everywhere earth's shrill delight
Shakes and shimmers through the night,
Silver tides of music flow
'Round the world; the cricket's low
Harp, the starry ecstasy
Of the keen cicadas' cry
With "I love, I love, I love,"
To the cloudless moon above
Lifts the old, the endless song,
And the firefly among
The low boughs and heavy leaves

22

THE MOONLIGHT SONATA

His hushed flight in silence weaves:
Deeper than the love they sing,
The unutterable thing,
The sheer pang wherewith he glows,
Burns his body as he goes.

Now earth draws the trembling veil
From her bosom cloudy pale,
And the bridegroom of the night
Flows to her in solemn light—
Memories of the absent sun
Dreaming of his lovely one.

From that fiery embrace
Wearied out, with lifted face,
Tangled hair, and dewy eyes,
Drowsed and murmurous she lies
In the bride-sleep, the deep bliss
After some exalted kiss,
Swooning through the darkness dim;
Still with memories of him
Her hushed breath comes fierce and low,
And the love that thrilled her so
Speaks in slumber, from her lips
The deep word of longing slips.

23

THE MOONLIGHT SONATA

Fragrant is thy flowery hair,
O belovèd, everywhere
Thy faint odour on the air,
From dread arches of thy grace
Wafted, what dark, secret place
Of dusk tresses in the wild
Midnight of thy locks beguiled,
Beckoning vistas of thy sheer
Maddening loveliness, the dear
Curves of thy bright beauty, all
Lure me to wild love:—the call
Of past lives is in my breast,
Premonitions, dimly guessed,
Of seraphic, solemn things,
Mingled lips and murmurings
On cool nights that gave me birth.
Yet, O mother, awful earth!
What stark mystery no less
Breaks the bosom that I press
Close against thy carelessness.

Where the holy poem of night
In veiled music and moonlight,
Shimmering cries and stars and dreams,
Onward in soft rhythm streams,

With reluctant pulse and pause
To its lovely ending draws
Thy long passion, when unroll
The starred heavens, like a scroll,
The old parable and story,
Some transcendent allegory—
Mother, mother, yet I know
Of cool nights that whispered so
When I was not, long ago!
When thy beauty, murmuring low,
With abandon, like a bride,
Throws her glimmering veils aside,
The dread love I dare not say
Turns my trembling lips away,
Something deeper, something more
Than I ever guessed before,
A new homesickness at heart
Hungering for the home thou art;
As the rivers to the one
Sea with solemn longing run,
So my being to thy breast,
So my sorrow to thy rest.

Thou art mother, thou art bride,
By what dearer name beside

Must I name thee, must I call,
Who art dearer far than all?

On thy heart I lay my head—
O what is it thou hast said!—
Secret, beautiful and dread—
Lovely moment drawing near—
Thought, most terrible and dear:
To be one with thy complete
Dark, sweet loveliness, my sweet,
One with thy wild will again—
To descend in rushing rain
To thy ravished breast, to pour
Through the veins that I adore,—
Drink deep draughts of thee, and grow,
Through long love and longing, so
Into the belovèd, flow
In thy deepest pulse, at home
In the dark and silent loam
Drenched with thee, and tremble up
In the lily's lifted cup—
Odours, clouds, and starry haze,
Breath of the wet country ways
On cool, moon-clear, fragrant nights;
Or where thy supreme delight's

THE MOONLIGHT SONATA

Radiant passion draws aghast
Sobs of thunder through the Vast—
Shuddering breath and murmur of
Thy fierce wrath of sullen love—
Laughter of thy mingling heart—
In thy lifted lightnings dart
Through awed heaven's glimmering bound,
With bright laughter all around,
With dark tears into the ground
Glide, and slake with loving rain
The parched caverns of thy pain!

Rapturous bridal! O wild heart!
To be part of thee, a part
Of this holy beauty here—
Sacred sorrow drawing near!
Sweet surrender—O my sweet,
Longingly my pulses beat—
Dazzling thought and fearful of
The dear fury of thy love—
Even now that draws me down,
My faint body to thine own,
Near and nearer yet, till I
Tangled in thy being lie,
Close and close, for sheer excess

Wearied out with loveliness:
All this little self, this me,
Soothed into the self of thee,
Rendered up in ecstasy!

Almost now thou seem'st to steal
From my breast the self. I feel
How my being everywhere,
As in dream, upon the air
Widens 'round me, till I grow
All I look on, overflow—;
And into the life adored
All the life of me is poured,
Through warm portals of thy heart
Drifting gently where thou art,
Who art all things, in the breeze
Stirring all the tangled trees
To low whispers, how I pass
Through each tiny blade of grass,
Tremble in moonlight, and rise
Looking out of other eyes—
Mystery of mysteries!
Pang of self, and tragical
Birth into the enlightened All—
O dark rapture—to flow, press,

Cease into thy loveliness,
With exalted weariness
Render up myself, and be,
Selfless, the dear self of thee,
In divine oblivion
One with the belovèd one!

Where I press my burning face
Weeds and grasses interlace:
Sweetheart, are these dewy, soft
Tears for me, who must so oft
Perish of thee to be thine?
Deep I drink of you, divine
Dizzy draught, bewildering wine!

In the grass my head is bowed.
The vague moon is in a cloud.
From my breast I feel it stream,
All I loved so, like a dream—.
Ah, I cannot understand,
But the wind is like a hand
On my forehead in caress,
And the earth is tenderness,—
Holy, grave, and very wise—
The deep tears are in her eyes;

29

THE MOONLIGHT SONATA

While around her sleeplessly
Shrills the restless will-to-be.
Passion for eternity
Shakes in sound, and floats in light
Through the darkness.   Through the night
Clouds, and dreams, and fireflies,
And my songs of her arise.

DAWN ON MID-OCEAN

VEILED are the heavens, veiled the throne,
    The sacred spaces of the vast
And virgin sea make sullen moan
    Into the Void whence God has passed.

With His right hand He wakened it,
    The sorrowing Deep, to sweet dismay,—
And sighed; with His left hand He lit
    The stars in heaven, and took His way,

Leaving this loveliness behind:
    The inconsolable Vacancy
Bears witness in the veiled night and blind
    To some departed Mystery.

Disconsolate for One withdrawn,
    Moan the vague mouths. One cold and clear
Star, like a lamp, in the pale dawn
    Trembles for passion: God was here!

DEAR EARTH

DEAR Earth, thy soft and murmurous voice I hear,
Thy drowsy cry of inarticulate love
Drawing me downward to thy breast, above
Thy drowsy breast I bend in joy and fear.

Fragrant and dewy are thy locks, dread bliss
Breathes from thy body's arches. Sweet, I kneel,
And all the senses from my spirit steal.
Upon thy breasts I lay my reverent kiss.

But look—the hand of moonlight for a fleet
Moment the dim and cloudy veil divides—
Glimmers thy holy body like a bride's—
My beautiful,—my dark-eyed love,—my sweet!

Darling, deep of thy dewy tears I drink,—
Too fain of thee, alas, too full of thee,
Faints of thyself my being utterly—
Sweetheart, into thine arms in death I sink.

GOLDEN NOON

NOW part the heavens in cloudless glory,
  And the wide eye of the world's light
Reopens, like a flower dilating,
  And floods the world with golden might.

Rose of the heaven! Heavy flower
  In the clean meadows of the sky!
Shed forth the odour of thy splendour,
  Thy dazzled perfume from on high.

The massive thunder of thy music
  Makes holy harmonies afar,
The starry mouths are mute before thee,
  O sumptuous and sovereign star!

Great chords of light, gigantic, shaken
  With heavy vibrance and immense—
The gorgeous trumpets of thy zenith
  And noon of thy magnificence!

Though soundless to the sensual hearing,
  With sonant light thrilled through and through—

GOLDEN NOON

Thine awful and august desire
    On horns of gold blown down the Blue!

Priest of the world, in radiance folded
    And veils of blue Immensity!
Shed thy triumphant light before us
    And trail thy robes across the sea.

Shadows and star-beams fly before thee,
    The level floors of the blue Vast
With lapse of trampling waves adore thee,
    And the soft twilight thrills aghast.

Like phantoms, or like ghosts, dividing
    Before thy forehead's flame, they flee—
Darkness and dreams in shifting hollows,
    And shadow-clouds across the sea,

When on the wave of morning steering
    Breaks 'round the world thy steady prow;
In rosy foam of light unfolding
    Heaven's billowing deeps dissolve. But now

The mellow fields lie hushed and helpless
    Beneath thy most enormous might,

GOLDEN NOON

And the crushed earth bleeds oozy color
    And golden drippings of thy light

Beneath that steady weight and wonder,
    Thy ponderous glory over all.
What solemn silence goes before thee
    Where all the woods were musical!

O Father! Though I may not see thee,
    Nor save through tears to thy blurred face
Lift up mine eyes, O blurred and golden!
    Hear now my prayer, and grant me grace.

Pour through my heart thy cleansing fire,
    That only is unknown of thee—
Make broad my breast as the horizon,
    And spacious as the sunlit sea;

Till all my life is searched and riven
    With eager ardor of thine own:
Till from horizon to horizon
    And blazing zone to blazing zone

The trumpets of thy light are sounded,
    And the wide heavens clear of gloom,
Clean-swept, are blinded and bedazzled,
    And bared for thee one radiant room!

MOONLIT EARTH

THE quiet earth in cool felicity,
  With listless lips that all day long implored
  Rest of the sun, her lover and her lord,
Sleeps in the moonlight of his memory:
Though far from her, though vanished utterly
  Down fiery spaces, still his love is poured
  Backward in dream upon the most adored,
With holy moonlight haunting land and sea.

Still to that heart of darling love he yearns
  Homeward in light, while from lost yesterday
  Upon her face his lonely kisses fall;
Remembering, remembering, he returns
  To the dear place, and sheds from far away
  The moonlight of his memory over all.

SUMMER DAWN

HERE, in the pallid chamber, where I lie,
    Out of the hungry hollows of the night
There comes a sombre and an ancient cry—
Dawn flowers up along the windy sky,
    Immense and white.

Laughable sadness fills me silently:
    Ever unto my spirit, whip-poor-will,
You are the wail of days that used to be,
The voice of my lost childhood calling me
    Beyond the hill.

DEPARTURE

ONE last look, and then—farewell to you forever,
    Room that I have loved, dearest place of all!
Softly through the window pours the lonely moonlight
    Slumbers on the bed, slumbers on the wall.

Faint in glimmering fields the grasshoppers are shrilling
    As on nights of old, and a cricket, too,
Bravely his one note drones solemnly and slowly,—
    Branches in the light droop all drenched with dew.

Here is the low table where we laughed together,
    Chairs, where we have sat, huddle side by side:
In the quiet night-time the old house is musing
    Deep on vanished days, and old dreams that died.

Where my youth has sorrowed now lies only moonlight,
    —Moonlight on the bed—moonlight on the floor—,
And across the pillow where your head lay dreaming,
    O my lost belovèd,—moonlight evermore—.

II

APRIL LIGHTNING

In the harsh world of effort and of pain
And many a buffet rude, the lands of death
And fierce survival, see,—in the little room
Sits the one kind, the one consoling thing—
Where your belovèd with brave beauty dear,
Frail body swaying, and laughing lips of love,
Lures your sad heart to the most fugitive joy.

APRIL LIGHTNING

I

APRIL was in the air,
    Your sweet lips whispered, "Take!"
Bravely you bade love's will
    Be done for love's own sake.

The Spring was full of kindness,
    And the heaven in your eyes,—
Bravely you bowed and accepted
    Spring's loveliest sacrifice.

And all your life in flower,
    Dear, to my very own,
As the meadows to the Springtime,
    Lay graciously overthrown.

II

MY sweet is a thief; all life, all love, all song,
 From the loved breast into her own she steals—
Life hastens unto the breast where life belongs,
 As a faint moth that toward a flower reels.

Her body's vehement loveliness and light
 All joy, all love, all hope, all song, all power,
To be wasted across the chalice of her life,
 Lures with soft beauty, like an unfolding flower.

Love is her beauty's slave that she compels
 To be wasted upon her sweetness night and day—,
O Loveliness lures Love to die for her,
 Beauty lures Love to give himself away!

III

O THRILL to the core of my pulses,
    Dear, with your very own!
Let me drink in around me
    No self but yours alone,—

Feel you, and breathe you, and live you,
    Till the penetrant loveliness
Even to the deep core
    Pervade me and possess!

Till quickened and drenched with your spirit,
    Saturate through and through,
I tremble into your being,
    Myself no more,—but *you!*

IV

LOVELY night that drawest near,
    Thou art terrible and dear,—
With the thought of thee at noon,
Sweet and dread, my senses swoon.

With the thought of the dear might,
Her bared beauty in the night,
That fierce sweetness unsubdued,
Her wild ways in wayward mood.

O my own, what must be done
For thy sake, belovèd one,
Ere the morning, to fulfill
The young ardors of thy will!

My blood trembles, my heart's beat
Shakes, the life of me, my sweet,
To thy life lies overthrown,
That must give thee all his own.

Idly the long hours stray,
The long twilight of the day

Faints, and dies for sheer excess
Of the evening's loveliness!.

In the self beloved he gives
All his self away—and lives:
Nearer is the hour sped,
The dear beauty, dark and dread.

So my spirit utterly
Faints for thee, and dies of thee,
That must be, ere morning shine,
One with thee, and wholly thine.

V

IN that moment,
  Before at your heart I surrendered myself completely,
Long, long did I look
On the dear and the inexorable face;
And as one about to die
Might salute the conqueror, so I kissed it,
Bowing my head, and heard
The voice of Life from your breast calling, calling
To the bright doom.

VI

O YOU are wise in many things,
　　Between your languid breath and breath
Heaves with a thousand murmurings
　　The tidal pulse of life and death.

All my desire, how vain it is,
　　And all desire—ah, how vain
You know, yourself have felt the kiss,
　　The barren pleasure, and the pain;

And smilingly, as from a height,
　　You look upon me far below—
And half in pity, half in fright,
　　Lean down your lips, and touch me, so.

VII

SWEET, why will you still refuse,
　　Still refrain, and still delay!
Bow—and let the old kindness, dear,
　　Be done in the old way.

Bow your head, and let the brave
　　Miracle of the insistent Spring
Pass, and be done between our lips,
　　Here at our hearts that cling.

VIII

NOW, the stars of twilight
    One by one depart—,
Still your heart in slumber
    Trembles at my heart.

O the darling beauty,
    Helpless as in death!
Love, for reverent rapture,
    Hardly dares draw breath

Lest his breathing wake you
    Into grief again—,
Lovely is the burden,
    Lovely is the pain.

Nightlong will I bear it,
    Sleepless, at my breast,
Not to stir your slumber—,
    Not to break your rest.

IX

EVEN as the rose her beauty, flower by flower,
    So Life sheds love with rapture, breath by breath;
Blossoming deathward, we give ourselves away
    At the dear breast: Love is the path to Death.

But the sweet Springtime body lures and lures;
    Even as the flowers, our very youth of May
We render up at the belovèd breast,
    At the dear breast that steals it all away.

X

IF, reborn, you return
　　To the earth as a boy,
As a girl will I come
　　To renew the old joy.

O the eager boy-face—
　　The dear eyes not unknown—
The sweet, opposite strength
　　That makes war on my own!

What grace will I give you,
　　What bounteousness,
And all the kind joy
　　And the love I possess—

In the Spring, in the Spring,
　　When the hawthorne is white,
In the midsummer night,
　　In the silence of night,

As you give me them now—,
　　Though the lips be above,

51

Or the lips be below,
    They shall greet you with love!

But if as a girl
    You return to the earth,
As a boy will I pass
    Through the portals of birth;

Still ever to be
    Through all cycles of breath,
Through the soft revolutions
    Of life and of death,

Your opposite ever,
    Your fate and dear foe—,
Though the lips be above,
    Or the lips be below.

XI

WHEN your eyes are closed in love
    Softlier than soft lids in death
Sealed forever, when your bosom
    Heaves with the resistless breath,—

Ah, when beauty is overthrown,
    The breast shudders, the heart sighs,
Bending over them I behold,
    Closed as in death, your love-closed eyes!

XII

WITH what fierce and holy longing,
　　With what ecstasy of pain,
Toward each other that we need so,
　　Sweet, we rush, we haste again!

From the fountain-heads of beauty,
　　From the well-springs of delight
With fierce rapture rearisen,
　　Each on each, as day and night

For the opposite dear other
　　Thirsting, with immortal pain
Slakes the loneliness of being
　　In the self beloved again.

XIII

SO utterly did I adore thee
 That darling night in dear embrace,
Out of myself my longing bore me
 To the lost home, the longed-for place:
And I became thee, my soul wore thee
 As her own body, for a space!

XIV

I DREAMED I passed a doorway
    Where, for a sign of death,
White ribbons one was binding
    About a flowery wreath.

What drew me so I know not,
    But drawing near I said,
"Kind sir, and can you tell me
    Who is it here lies dead?"

Said he, "Your most belovèd
    Died here this very day,
That had known twenty Aprils,
    Had she but lived till May."

Astonished I made answer,
    "Good sir, how say you so!
Here have I no belovèd,
    This house I do not know."

Quoth he, "Who from the world's end
    Was destined unto thee

Here lies, thy true belovèd,
    Whom thou shalt never see."

I dreamed I passed a doorway
    Where, for a sign of death,
White ribbons one was binding
    About a flowery wreath.

XV

LOVE, for the world your pity, or the gay
  Moods of your careless and abundant grace,
  The language of the laughter of your face
And lips of luring all the livelong day.

But, sweet, for me in the lost night and lone
  The sacred frenzy of your breast of love
  Where the inexorable ardors move,
And lips, all quivering, salt against my own!

XVI

LET me here at your heart weep out my woe,
  All the wild shame, dear, and the nameless grief,
  Till the long sigh that brings the soul relief
Sink back, and sorrow into silence flow.

Where should I turn to, if not here, for rest—
  Or sorrow save at the source of sorrow bare?
  But O the gulf 'twixt spirit and spirit there—
Alone at your heart I lie, alone at your breast,

While the lost love droops dead between! Too well
  I know there is no loathlier hell than this,
  Than the cold touch of the first loveless kiss;
But the tears fail us at the heart of hell.

O only once, 'mid all the thirst of the years,
  To glut grief at the bosom that might make
  His heaven yet, and the whole heart to slake
Once only with the wanton waste of tears!

XVII

THE weary joy and the familiar peace
　　Wherewith we close, after long leagues of strife,
　　Is older and more sorrowful than life.

Up the sharp scale of beauty passion runs,
　　And sinks, after the rapture and the pain,
　　Into the grave and general doom again.

XVIII

I DO not love to see your beauty fire
 The light of eager love in every eye,
Nor the unconscious ardor of desire
 Mantle a cheek when you are passing by;
When in the loud world's giddy thoroughfare
 Your holy loveliness is noised about—
Lips that my love has prayed to—the gold hair
 Where I have babbled all my secrets out—

O then I would I had you in my arms,
 Desolate, lonely, broken, and forlorn,
Stripped of your splendor, spoiled of all your charms;
 So that my love might prove her haughty scorn—
  So I might catch you to my heart, and prove
  'Tis not your beauty only that I love!

XIX

I THOUGHT of you when in the pallid dawn
    Glimmered day's loveliest and loneliest star,
Infinitely in the pale blue withdrawn,
    Touching my heart with beauty from afar;
Where bending with her blossoms the white spray,
    After the passing of a sudden shower,
Trembled all dewy in the wind of May—
    I thought of your white loveliness in flower.

And once in the deep wonder of a dream
    You came to me, and your clear face was bowed
Over my face, like light on a dark stream,
    And your soft hair fell 'round me like a cloud;
      And then I woke—but still, when you were gone,
      Like music in my heart you lingered on.

XX

'TIS not your darling loveliness alone
    That draws me, the proud splendor of your face,
Beautiful as a conqueror's on his throne,
    Or a swift runner's in an eager race;
Not that carved throat, that chalice of sweet sound,
    Nor eyes that are the heavens of my prayer,
Pale, perfect brows from many a conquest crowned
    Victorious, nor the halo of your hair.

These the dull crowd gape after, little they
    Guess the still lovelier being hid from view,
The pilgrim in this prison-house of clay,
    Which is yourself, the very soul of you—
        Whose banner Love here flings to heaven unfurled,
        And bares his shining sword to all the world!

XXI

LIFE let me squander and lavish
    Recklessly, without rest,
And waste myself forever
    At the belovèd breast—
As Night at the heart of Morning,
    To become her, gives up breath—
Faint, as at Song's heart Silence,
    Lost, as at Life's heart Death!

XXII

FROM my own lips I drink your tears;
　　Their taste is bitterer than gall.
　　Is this the end, the end of all?

Is this the summit of your beauty,
　　Your beauty's beauty have I had?
　　O sweet, and yet I am not glad!

XXIII

AH, never in all my life
Have I ever fled away
From the loneliness that follows
My spirit night and day.

Though I fly to the dearest face,
It follows without rest—
To the kind heart of love
And the belovèd breast.

Though I walk among the crowd,
Still I walk apart:
Alone, alone I lie
Even at the loved one's heart!

XXIV

WHEN the old evening was slowly growing gray
  My restless heart would leave me in peace no more,
And I arose and wandered far, far away,
  As I had done a thousand times before.

And when I had wandered far, far away,
  I lifted up my hands in loneliness once more,
And prayed with all my heart, until I could not pray,
  As I had done a thousand times before.

I prayed with all my heart, until I could not pray,
  For what I knew could be never, never more,
And rose up in bitterness, and slowly came away—
  As I had done a thousand times before.

XXV

AGAIN the weary longing
 Cries out in me for rest,
That dreads, and yet desires
 The oblivion of your breast.

Alas, too well he knows it—
 There is no other way—
Again he must die to love you,
 As darkness dies of day.

For pity's sake be cruel—
 Lean down your lips again,
And give him the kind death, dear,
 That puts an end to pain!

XXVI

THE shivering and shining waters move
    Under a low moon in the windy sky,
The stars hang pale and breathless far above—
O to be killed here by the things I love,
    To mix with all this beauty, and to die!

XXVII

GIVE me your pitiful, soft hand, and lay
     Your cheek against my shoulder—let your head
   Rest heavily, and your loose hair be shed
Where the heart breaks with what it cannot say:
Springtime is in the air, the winds of May
     Rustle the silken curtains, and are fled—
     Give me your hand—ah, let no word be said—
Let the great will of silence have its way!

You do not love me.   And at last I know
     How far lies the lost land for which I pine;
          But in the lonely passion of my mood
I feel your pulses toward my pulses flow,
     And the dear blood that through your hand to mine
          Whispers her pity in the solitude.

XXVIII

WHY wilt thou bow thine heart to mine, and shed
  Wild tears for me, as for one already dead?—
 Alas—and am I already dead to thee—
O sweet, at thine heart, here at thy living breast,
Am I already only one with the rest,
  A ghost, a memory!

XXIX

YOU were the instrument on which I played,
    Such heavenly music from your heart I wrung
And echo, where on the strings my fingers strayed,
    Of a new song that never yet was sung!

Now you have left me, dear, how shall I bear,
    When lesser hands over the chords are moved
Of that most exquisite instrument, to hear
    All harsh and jangled the great song I loved?

XXX

UNDER your window, deep in the heart of the night,
  Something is crying under the starry sky,
Between the going night and the growing light,
  It is I, it is I.

Under your window cries without quiet or rest,
  Something that cries, with the hurrying winds that cry,
For the *you* that sleeps deep in the heart of your breast;
  It is I, it is I.

XXXI

WHEN I had need of you, you would not hear;
Now that amid the anguish and the smart
You turn to me, to the last crack of doom
I will not fail,—O dear and careless heart!

XXXII

ONLY yesterday these eyes
    Drank your loveliness that here
Breathed and trembled—now it lies
    All in dust, that beauty dear:

In the darkness of the grave
    Broken, broken, spoiled, and spent,—
Like an unavailing wave,
    On death's shore in discontent!

No farewell you made, nor said
    Aught in leaving us, but bright,
Careless, and disdainful, fled
    Back into the lonely night.

Like a flash of lightning fleet,
    Blinding the soft sky of Spring,
Was your beauty—O so sweet,
    And so swiftly vanishing!

XXXIII

THE thought of you is woven through the Springtime
    Like a sad minor in the pæan of Joy;
I cannot see the Spring and quite forget,
Nor is the Springtime anymore the same.

You were the tenderness of her wide hills,
The patient longing and the wistfulness
Of all her tremulous blossoms on the air
Gently unfolded for the first, sweet time,
—Her trustful loveliness in mute appeal.

Each year repeats my sorrow but anew:
When autumn darkens o'er the solemn lands,
To me it is as if again I see
Upon the face the most beloved on earth,
The rapture and Springtime once of all my life,
The first, sad lines of shame and sorrow there,
Stealing its whole brave loveliness away.

XXXIV

SUCH flowers as I brought to you in life
   I bring you now to lay upon your grave,
Now all your dear defiances are dust,
   And all your beauty broken, like a spent wave.

O swift and sweet and most untameable,
   What pity should I bring you now to grieve you!
Ah, though from love you hid away your face
   Deep in the dark, yet love will never leave you.

Now is all memory of you wiped away
   Out of all men forevermore, and yet,
O foolish heart and most adorable,
   Though none remember, I will not forget!

XXXV

NOT your heart's kingdom did I abdicate
    Where royally in splendor I had reigned,
  Nor base admittance, nor consignment deigned
When the usurper hammered at the gate;
But heavily and to the hand of Fate
    Love bowed his head, to this extreme constrained—
  While deeplier his dying life-blood stained
The regal purple of the robes of state.

Then through the outer court there ran a word,
    And from the throng a mighty murmuring
Broke on his soul, in pangs of death deferred
    And anguish of supremest suffering,
And far away a fading voice he heard,
    Crying "The King is dead.   Long live the King!"

XXXVI

IN dreams you come to mock me, in deep night,
 When dark is all the earth and slumber-still,
Save for the streaming of the pale starlight
 And far-off wailing of the whip-poor-will.

Then through the room that held you once you move
 With the old carelessness and dear disdain,
And lift your hands up in the way I love—
 And the old ritual we repeat again.

Still from your lips that secret I entreat—
 The riddle still unanswered evermore—
And to your lips your finger-tip in sweet
 Command you lift and silence, as before;

And in the pallor of the waning night,
 Laughing, but silently, you fade away:
And morning glimmers, and the feeble light
 Widens into the common blaze of day.

XXXVII

STELLA we called you, you whose young joy shed
    Light, starry bright, on these dark ways below;
Now that her fire lies quenched among the dead,
    "Stella," we think, "bright star set long ago."

XXXVIII

YOUR loveliness was like a wave,
    The sudden stroke of her delight
Flooded my heart's adoring cave:
    The shock of the belovèd might
    Startled the gloom to starry light,
That gave it back, and drank, and gave.

But broken, broken is her strength,
    That vehement glory loved before,
The sweet rage of her radiant length
    Shattered and shed forevermore:
        The adorable ardor, the dear might,
        Hurled itself deathward with delight,—
And sank upon the sounding shore.

III

THE AWAKENING DUST

God is all things everywhere,
In Mind He wakes from slumber deep—
Man is His eternal prayer,
And the dust is God asleep.

THY KINGDOM COME!

NOW in the east the morning dies,
    The full light of the splendid sun
Strikes downward on our lifted eyes
    And the long journey is begun:
        Across the shattered walls
        A voice prophetic calls,
        With tumult and with laughter
        We rise and follow after.

The modern world, immense and wide,
    Awaits us, huger than before,
With new stars swimming in the Void,
    And Science broadening evermore
        The sweep of the limitless Vast,
        The Past is dead and past;
        Yet through it all forever
        One voice is silent never.

'Mid iron wheels and planets whirled,
    The clanging city, in the street,
—The machinery of the modern world—
    His lips cry loudly and entreat,

THY KINGDOM COME!

Like one that lifts his head
For a second time from the dead,
—Out of the Ages' prison
The new Christ re-arisen!

O holy spirit—O heart of man!
Will you not listen, turn, and bow
To that clear voice, since time began
Loud in your ears, and louder now!
Mankind, the Christ, retried—
Recrowned, recrucified;
No god for a gift God gave us,
Mankind alone must save us.

Will you not hear him—reach your hand!—
From factory, tenement and slum
His voice pleads vainly in the land,
Ah, heart of man, the time has come!
The voice of Cain that wailed
Grew sorrowful and failed,
But a new voice rings deeper,
"You *are* your brother's keeper."

O world, grown pitiless and grim!
O world of men, had you but known

THY KINGDOM COME!

Your brother is your Christ, through him
　　You must be saved and him alone!
　　　　Love for his sorrows—love
　　　　Alone can lift you above
　　　　The pain of your misgiving,
　　　　The doom and the horror of living.

Within ourselves we must find the light
　　And in ourselves our gods to-be,
Not throned beyond the stars of night;
　　Here, in America, we must see
　　　　The love of man for man,
　　　　The new world republican,—
　　　　A heaven, not superhuman,
　　　　Reborn in man and woman.

Forward—!　Truth glorifies, not kills
　　The ancient marvel of the soul,
Each new progression but fulfills
　　That wonder,—the wheels of the world that roll
　　　　Thundering, but proclaim
　　　　God with a louder name;
　　　　Science, revealing, rehearses
　　　　But vaster universes.

THY KINGDOM COME!

Though the dark veil of dusk and doom
    You strip from off the Soul of things,
Though with new torches through the gloom
    You hunt Him on untiring wings,
        And in the starry space,
        You shall not find His face;
        A voice comes following after
        Out of the dust with laughter.

The Vision—the Ideal—the God—
    Not anything ever may destroy.
Then let us follow, winged and shod
    With love, with courage and with joy;
        Herein alone is the truth,
        The glory and fire of youth,
        Herein all high endeavor,
        Forever and forever!

FROM A TRANSPORT

LAND calls to land, and on the huddled hills
　　Of field and city many a sound is heard
Of horn and whistle, motor and gong afar;
But we must follow down the trackless path
Of the unfurrowed and abundant sea,
Over the mute road of unending waves,—
The desert of the Deep, divine and sad,
Where between daylight and dim starlight blows
Immensity, which is the breath of God,
Between earth's warring nations ringed around.

THE FAR LAND

WE are sighing for you, far land—
    We are praying for you, far land,
All our life long, working, waiting, night and day:
    But as waves that die to reach the farther shore
    Break our hearts that die to reach you evermore—
    All our hearts are breaking, breaking toward that shore,
O far land, so near and far away!

    At the lips of the belovèd,
    At the breast of the belovèd,
Like waves that seek the land, and sink forlorn—
    O to reach it we have died, but to that beach
    Where the belovèd is love may not reach!
    Our children's children even shall not reach
The far land where all of us were born.

    Through the terror of the ages
    We have sought it, till the ages
Have stamped our lifted faces with our love:
    But long though we have wandered, where we are
    The far land is not.   O that land is far!

THE FAR LAND

Beyond the night, beyond the morning-star
The far land grows further as we move.

In music and in story,
In song and sacred story
We yearned to it, in color and in sound:
But swifter than the soul the secret flies,
The vision pales—beyond, beyond it lies,
Beyond all songs, beyond all harmonies,
The far land that we have never found.

In the sweat of daily labor,
In the anguish of our labor
We strove to bind it fast in steel and stone:
But lo—the walls were dust, the work was naught,
And O it was not what the heart had sought!
'Twas something dearer that our blood had bought—
The far land that we have never known.

Beyond long sea-horizons,
Beyond sad sea-horizons
Our furrowing keels have wandered in that quest;
Beyond the sunset, tremulous and dear,
Glimmered that land, but as our prows drew near

THE FAR LAND

Faded the dream, the far land is not here,
The far land, the home-land of the breast.

So we built ourselves a heaven,
Our God we set in heaven,
With prayer and praise we wrought them to our will:
But they could not fill the measure of our love
For the far land—O they were not great enough!
There is nothing, there is nothing great enough!
The far land is something greater still.

We are sighing for you, far land—
We are dying for you, far land,
In the trenches, in the bloody ruck and blind.
We are coming, we are coming, every breath
Is a wave that bears us nearer to you, death
Seals our cry. O might our children find ere death
The far land that we have died to find!

LITANY

FAINT as the murmuring of a widowed crone
  That mourns one memory forevermore,
(Now that she sees it all—O now at last!)
Hark—in the church the thin voice of the World,
Repeating sad, repentant words, and slow,
For the old murder of her patient Christ.
O now she sorrows for Him—hark—how soft . . .
Who loved her in her youth, when all her breast
Was strong and cruel as a laughing girl's.

EAGLES OF DEMOCRACY

CHAPMAN gone, and Lufbery flown his last brave flight
      to the farthest place!—
Bow your head for the dauntless dead—in grief and glory
      lift up your face—
Raise a shout to the winds about, to voice the triumph of
      all the Race!

Yes, for still what the human will may dare to dream of
      the strange and new,
Still we find the hand and the mind to dare the devil, and
      see it through—
The hand and the brain to dare the pain, till doubt be slain
      and the dream come true.

Cæsar's pride may debar and divide men's hearts from men
      with the spears of war,
These are brothers that make all others brothers and lovers
      from shore to shore—
Man, not men, one spirit again in the struggle Godward
      forevermore.

EAGLES OF DEMOCRACY

Each in the Race, not each in his place, the king and the
    beggar, the sage and the clod,
Lives or dies, must sink or rise; on the road of the ages that
    Man has trod
All together we brave the weather—the upward march of
    the soul toward God.

Though to the earth, whence we all have birth, their bodies
    sank when the worst was done,
Not with these down the baffled breeze their souls sank,
    soaring beyond and on,
Upward ever, and on forever, till all the glory of all be won.

Hail, all hail, in the beating gale still battling onward against
    the blast!
The motors hum and the stars cry "Come—." Hail! All
    hail! And farewell at last—
Song would follow, but sinks back hollow and worn with
    winging the windy Vast.

THE WORLD-SORROW

IN dreams I found Her, by the crimson tide
   Of the world's tumult throned,—awful and still:
  Her sloping breast was like a slumbrous hill,
Or mighty forest where all winds have died.
There was no pity in Her face, nor pride,
   But flawless grief, and the unflinching will
   Of sorrow, voiceless and supreme, did thrill
My reckless heart to reverence long denied.

And to that dreadful and oblivious breast
My songless lips and dreamless heart I pressed,
   And felt, in the large calm of Her embrace,
The perfect and inexorable Truth
Humble with hallowing hands my grieving youth
   Into the shoreless grief of all the race.

HYMN OF MAN, 1917

O NOW to Thee, who art our God,
   We lift our voices crying,
"For the long path that must be trod
   Give us a faith undying!"
     The years and ages roll,
     Still steadfast stands the soul:
     Strong love and flawless faith,
     Triumphant over death,
       Not anything shall conquer.

Give us the victory, O Lord,
   Not beggarlike we cower—
Man's will is his own holy sword,
   Within us is the power.
     The sad and sacred doom
     That bears us to the tomb
     Makes humble not our lives,
     More undefeated strives
       The God within us Godward.

No less than what we will, we can—
   The ages shall fulfill it—

Man is the highest hope of Man,
   If he but only will it:
      Though prophecy be dumb,
      Yet shall Thy kingdom come
      And not in heaven above,—
      On earth the reign of love
         'Twixt man and man shall bring it.

The centuries and the cycles groan
   Before Thy vast desire,
And all the starry heavens sown
   With everlasting fire;
      Lo—Thou art everywhere,
      In earth and sea and air,
      The spirit and the clod—
      In Man, too, dwells the God,
         And who shall crush, or kill it!

IV

THE SOURCE

> *Bewildered—rapturous—faint—*
> *Aghast, Life leans upon the breast of Love,*
> *At the⁻most holy and triumphant bosom,*
> *In the revealing moment.   With what pain,*
> *With what deep longing on the magnificent Breast,*
> *Beneficent, and eternal, and supreme,*
> *She leans her temporal beauty's sad, sweet weight!*
> *Ah, with what starriest longing all in vain*
> *Lies fugitive beauty against immortal Beauty—*
> *The life that dies at the breast of the Life eternal!*

OASIS

VAINLY for what I longed for
   I searched from east to west,
But ere my lips had spoken
   The belovèd heart had guessed.

Under the tree of Life
   She lured my heart aside,—
Ere my lips had spoken
   Silently she replied.

I leaned to her body's beauty,
   The radiant loveliness—,
Ere my lips had spoken
   Her beauty whispered *yes*.

With graciousness of pity
   Abundantly she shared
The bounty of her being,
   Her loveliness unbared,—

OASIS

The never-failing arms
And the sacrificial breast,
For a refuge in the desert
Of death from east to west.

REVELATION

FROM the bright form now glides the veil,
　　Leaving your slender beauty bare—
Your loveliness, extreme and frail,
　　Unfolds before me like a prayer
　　　　In tender silence, the supreme
　　　　Message of life, the wistful dream.

The source whither all being yearns
　　Glimmers revealed; the sacred source,
Toward which all life forever turns,
　　With secret and with subtle force
　　　　Lures me and draws me, sounds her clear
　　　　Challenge and invitation dear.

All for which love so blindly longs
　　Speaks in this presence; here is heard
The hymn of hymns, the song of songs,
　　Beauty's unutterable word
　　　　Beseeching the proud heart of Pain,
　　　　"Be born again, be born again!"

REVELATION

All joy, all wonder, all delight
    Of beauty in herself, is bared
Here at this breast, with exquisite
      Cunning for love's delight prepared,
        To weary life's rebellious cry
        The sovereign and serene reply—

Deftly with darling prescience wrought
    To pleasure the belovèd one,
A spur upon the tired thought
    Of life seeking oblivion,
      For the old hope's sake ceaselessly
      Compelling him again to be.

And I, that foolishly to Death
    So lately prayed that he might come,
The sweet and the persuasive breath
    Of very Life, calling me home,
      Through all my recreant pulses feel—
      The fragile splendor's mute appeal.

Ancient, inexorable, and wise,
    Through countless ages still the same,
To me the Eternal Kindness cries
    Out of this form, and puts to shame

REVELATION

My traitorous heart: all unexpressed
Passion sinks awed within the breast.

And can it be, this flawless flower,
  This frame of all dear bounties must
With every breath, with every hour
    Press toward the darkness?   Shall the dust
      Such awful tribute ask?   Ah, no—
      Eternal Pity, say not so.

Yet so it is.   Then am I proud
  That I the fate of all things fair
And brave, that in the dust have bowed
    Their darling heads in death, may share;
      For the first time since I drew breath
      I know the holy pride of death.

O Life, so insatiable, so dear—
  Sorrow resistless—for your sake
At the bright breast of being here
    Again I bow, again I take
      With solemn tears the lips of pain,
      Here die to be reborn again!

CHALLENGE

NEVER the woman's heart was all subdued,
　　Nor the last secret of it quite possessed;
Lovely and tireless, and a challenge still,
Laughingly, out of the weary arms of love
Virgin it rearises ever again—
Wayward, elusive, inviolable and fleet,
A tantalus and a fierce loveliness beyond.

REVERENCE

WHERE thy bosom draws profound
    The deep mystery of breath
The dark churchyard all around
    Slumbers in the dream of death.

In the heavings of thy breast,
    With resistless ebb and flow
Lifting, lapsing, without rest
    The sweet wave comes to and fro.

Where the inmost Awe sustains
    The dear being that thou art,
Where the sovereign Rhythm reigns
    In the palace of thy heart,

There I hear forevermore—
    Holy, tragic, and alone—
How life's sea with sullen roar
    Ebbs in awe to the Unknown.

REVERENCE

And I bow to thee, supreme
   Sumptuous splendor, flame that flies;
I adore thee, fragile dream—
   The deep tears are in my eyes.

WOMAN: BIRTH AND THE
RETURN THROUGH LOVE

BEAUTY, you are the flame the breath
   Of windy and unwilling Death
Quivers to quench, the battle-gage
Flung in his face with whom you wage
For us the immemorial strife
Of love, our champion of Life—
'Mid the dark terrors and profound
That girdle and enring us 'round,
O Loveliness, your flag unfurled
Is Life's lone banner in the world!

Your sweetness the proud heart of Pain
Beseeches to be born again
With promise of your loveliness
That lures him lifeward still, to press
Forward, nor faint, but for your sake
The ancient yoke and burden take
Renewed, the lonely and forlorn
Adventure; till, from you reborn,
Antares-like touching the earth

And holy well-head of our birth,
We, with the child's heart, reassume—
And lips of laughter through the gloom—
Our painful pilgrimage anew
Back to the mother-land of you.

Your pity falls like healing rain
On Life that brings to you again,
Still urgent evermore to be,
His prayer for immortality.
Ah, well enough you know the quest
That leads him backward to your breast—
Hearth of the Race, whereon the light
Of the world's fire is kept bright
Perpetually! Sacred spring,
From which we all are wandering,
Whither we all return at last
And, the long exile overpassed,
From mother to belovèd run
Love's orbit, till all love be done!

Our varying and veering will
Deserts you and desires still—
We are the wanderers, you, the home
Toward which we ever range and roam—

All we are wanderers, roam and range
The hills of chance, you know not change,
Keeping perpetually pure
The dream whereby we all endure.
O sacred well-head!   Fountain-sun!
O far land, wooed, yet never won,
And still beyond us!   Steady light,
That leads us wandering in the night!
Still we seek backward, still return—
The blind eyes brighten—yield and yearn
Our hungering hearts—from alien shores
The lost wave of the spirit pours
Homeward in passionate penitence
To the dear breast of Being, whence
Our children's children rearise
And seek you with the self-same eyes.

ADORATION

THOUGH Death and Time shall break you,
    There is a triumph here
In mortal things and human,
    In tragic things and dear.

—The shapely, stately splendour
    Of arms and breasts and hips,
And the defeated body,
    And the defiant lips—!

The patience of your passion,
    The grave and the gracious doom—,
Are holier than all gladness,
    And lovelier for the tomb.

O Beauty, holy Beauty,
    On whom the Eternal wars!
My choral adorations
    Shall echo to the stars.

ALL THE MORE

ALAS, dear love, how humbled sinks your head
    Before the beauty of the starry choir—
How suddenly is all your beauty fled
    Before the morning and the radiant Fire!

Pitiful are you, to the dusty doom
    Condemned, and to the sorrowful embrace
Your body hastens mournfully, the tomb
    Shall swallow up the sadness of your face;

And in the thought of the seraphic Wonder
    The thought of you sinks tired wings and tame—
The height and depth of beauty, over and under,
    Derides and puts your loveliness to shame.

The breathless awe of heaven, the white sleep
    Of star on star, makes you ridiculous,
Our love before the Love that thrills the Deep
    Fades, and the fiery wheels roll over us,

The holy, implacable wheels of all things moving
    Mercilessly forever.   All the more,

ALL THE MORE

Dearly belovèd, sorrowful and loving,
    I seek your bosom, with the world at war.

O sad and mortal! O most dear Desire,
    Holy and human, with the doom at strife!
Beneath the beauty of the starry choir
    I bow before you, at the throne of Life.

V

EARTH PUTS FORTH HER DREAM

Behold the tormented and the fallen angel,
  Wandering disconsolate the world along,
That seeks to atone with inconsolable anguish
  For some old grievance, some remembered wrong,—
To storm heaven's iron gates with angry longing,
  And beat back homeward in a shower of Song!

THE OPENING BARS OF
WAGNER'S "RING"

STEADILY Love begins to breathe and blow
    Into mute law sonorous life and strong;
The first breath of the giant labours slow
    To lift on his broad bosom all that song.

ERNEST DOWSON

O BROTHER, what is there to say to you,
　Now that your feet have passed beyond the sun!
　Now is the twilight waned, the dark begun,
And the consoling memories fall like dew.
Alas, what has your dreaming brought you to!
　O brother—what is this that you have done!
　But peace, these are no things to think upon,—
And evening brings the immortal stars to view.

As one might lay his palm upon your breast
　　And feel the pleading of your heart's demand,
　　　While yet it throbbed for life, though fain to weep;
Now, when the stars have gathered you to rest,
　　O inconsolable friend, I lay my hand
　　　Upon this page, and hear it, though you sleep.

SWINBURNE

NOT in some twilit temple of lights dying
  And meditative thought, in no far place
  Was he sequestered, whose exultant face
Was lifted in the broad daylight, defying,
Like his own ocean's thunder-throated crying,
  The lost, gone stars in the sun-circled space:
  A spirit girded up for a swift race,
And sent upon his purpose with no sighing.

Not throned amid the silence of some star
  Deep in the lonely coldness of the night,
But woven through the meadows near and far—
  A spirit laughing at his own delight,
  That veils his splendors in the sunset's light,
And moves like music through all things that are!

SHAKESPEARE'S JULIET: IN THE
VAULT OF THE CAPULETS

ALAS, what is this maiden-flower, full-blown,
    And wasted on the mournful marge of death—
  This Beauty, white with sleep, and out of breath,
That hurries toward the destiny unknown!
In the hushed tomb Love makes no humble moan,
    Triumphant over the silent face beneath
    Leaning, with tremulous lips and soul that saith
Forever, gloriously, one word alone.

O Juliet, your sorrow makes me glad,
    Seeing how Love and clamorous desire
      Through their own doom show grave and holiest,—
And Youth, unconquerable and never sad,
    Although it sink beneath the starry choir
      Silent, with all the music in its breast!

THE SEVENTH SYMPHONY

WHEN on the mind's wide-echoed wildernesses
    High music fades, and ever fainter roll,
Down endless sweeps and distant, dim abysses

Receding, the storm-voices of the soul,
    The spirit swoons out of the longing face.
O hungering face turned on an empty goal,

The vision is but vanished for a space,
    We are but banished for a little hour,
And set within this wild, unwilling place

By God, inexplicable, and God's power!
    But the vague voices grow more full and vast,
—The voice once dimly heard in field and bower;

Encompassing the long-lost arms at last,
    The old world-agonies fade down the Past.

LILITH

SHE loiters in low vallies lily-grown
    That open toward the ocean, and the tree,
    Wind-blown, whereon she leans in reverie,
Trembles to feel soft arms twined with its own.
Her smile is like a sigh—ah, were it known
    What stirred that smile so deep, so passionately,
    Dead sunsets, or the everlasting sea,
Or pale wistaria on the breezes blown!

And still she dreams, and still her pallid feet
    Crush the white lilies to the tender sod—
And still her heart with wild, attentive beat
    Throbs back the pleading passion of the sea,
    Regardless how along heaven's boundary
Flashes the thunder of an outraged God.

ROSSETTI

O MASTERLIEST sweet Heart, whose tight-tuned lyre
    Snaps at the one word, love,—and all along
  The vibrant chords a myriad memories throng,
Sudden with long-felt want and dumb desire!
Even to the utmost straining of each wire
    The numerous notes sound solemnly and strong;
    Deeper than this no modulate tones belong,
And than this note no notes reverberate higher.

Lay your hand on its pause, and let it pass—
    One thing too mastering for its heaviest strings
    And holiest. Deeper in the deep heart sings,
Tremulous as a weak wind on bowed grass,
    The innermost marvel of the soul of things,
And for it all no words—alas—alas!

BEETHOVEN

LONG ages ere the human dream began,
    From the dim dust, through flow'ret, leaf and stone,
  With slow persistance and laborious groan,
While the evolving stars their cycles ran,
Through monster and through beast reptilian,
    And the dumb brute with inarticulate moan,
    This spirit has moved upward to its throne
For a brief space, which was the body of Man.

And dwelling there, restless and discontent,
    'Prisoned a term in the repressive clod,
        Shed itself in a shower of shining sound;
So Beethoven the last progression went,
        Unto that high Supreme from this Profound—,
From Man, through Music, to concordant God.

TOLSTOI

LOOK on this face, and ponder on him well
    Who was the first to cleave the unknown seas!—
Upon this brow broke the new thought of the world
Whose waves we wander now with furrowing keel.

VI

BE BORN AGAIN!

Who shall lay bare love's inmost meaning, who
   Reveal the sovereign splendor on its throne,
   Or utter forth in language the unknown!—
Old is all language, but all love is new.
How may I tell you of this love that to
   Your bosom draws me from my very own.
   And wakes me to one need, and one alone,—
O love, the need to be reborn from you!

There is no word whereby love may declare
   His holy will ; but in the breathless deed
Of adoration, in the primal prayer
   At the belovèd breast, he tells his need
      To the one kind and conquering heart, and she
      In the great silence answers silently.

BE BORN AGAIN!

I

MY Love of you, like an angel,
　　Entered in my door,
To make his silent dwelling
　　Beside me evermore.

His eyes are deep and solemn,
　　His eyes are pure and grave—
Sacred to reprove,
　　And vigilant to save.

Across my singing of you
　　He leans a golden head,
Nightly, when I sleep,
　　He sits beside the bed.

He has your very lips,
　　Your forehead and your hair,
If I should awake,
　　Still I find him there.

BE BORN AGAIN!

II

O LOVE, now my life to yours in the moment of its
greatest need
Turns for the supreme compassion, and all my senses
pray
To your triumphant loveliness—O be great indeed
And gracious, as befits a conqueror—turn not my love
away!

But in the holy midnight of your tresses hide
My hunted soul from the arrows of your face. O let
me lie
Close, close at your breast, and against the solemn pride
Of your victorious heart hold close this heart that at
your own must die!

It faints for the land of your far beauty—O let it break
On the implacable silence of your bosom here!
Have pity on your lover—lay your arms about me for dear
pity's sake,—
Yet have no pity, pain itself from you is dear.

130

BE BORN AGAIN !

Hold me—O hold me close, that in the great moment I may
    know
    Your reassuring lips and breast that in the divine pas-
      sion move:
Be merciful as a victor to the vanquished in the hour of his
    overthrow,
    Merciful as death, and inexorable as love !

III

I CANNOT look on the face I love, for the many tears,
   Nor at the heart I love sing of the heart I love;
All the songs I had dreamed, where are they vanished away?
   All for the aching joy something sobs in the throat.

BE BORN AGAIN!

IV

FOR pity and compassion's sake
    Your holy beauty deigned to slake
My bitter need of you, the pain
That cried to you, and cried again.

To my prayer your loveliness
Whispered *yes* and whispered *yes*,—
To my need it made reply
Silently, silently.

And bravely still you lifted up
To my lips the brimming cup
Of your beauty, hushed and still,
And bade my longing have its will.

There was pity in your eyes
At my pleasure, sweet surprise
And friendly wonder, when you knew
First my utter love of you.

As one that barely understands,
But pities much, I felt your hands
Clinging, and around me thrown
Your kind arms, like a mother's own.

BE BORN AGAIN!

V

SOUL of all souls, like waves in the wild sea
    And ocean of all being, toward the shore
And massive limits of death's boundary
    Moving in trampled lapse forevermore—

Merge in my wrath, and let our mingled height,
    One instant foaming, catch with kindled crest
Life's glory;—and with sullen wrath of might
    Thunder in music on death's golden breast!

BE BORN AGAIN!

VI

WHAT is this memory, this homesickness,
    That draws me to yourself resistlessly,
  As to some far place where I long to be—
This exile's hungering for loveliness!
Here in the night the face that I caress
    Lies like a moonlit land beyond the sea.
    A kingdom lost, toward which the heart of me,
Shipwrecked and worn, beats backward in distress.

Have I been here before? How long ago,
    And on what pilgrimage and journey far
    Was lost this land remembered? By what star
Did I steer homeward? Only this I know,
That all my being from my breast would go
    To the dear home and heaven where you are.

BE BORN AGAIN!

VII

BEND over me, as if all heaven
    Leaned down to love me, let your hair
Fall 'round me, while, like stars at even',
    Your eyes shine in the twilight there—
        For a kind moment's happy space
        Crowd the whole world out with your face.

Now, looking up, I see above me,
    Through fluttering lashes golden-grave,
Your eyes, that almost seem to love me,
    Open in that sweet way they have
        Like flowers, your faint lips half-apart
        Make feverish music in my heart.

What sorrow can get in between us
    Here where your tresses shut away
Longing and loneliness, and screen us
    From all less beautiful than they
        Shut out, shut in with you alone
        Here, in this heaven all your own!

Not the whole world with all its treasure
    Has anything to give that is

BE BORN AGAIN!

So dear, so darling beyond measure,
    So marvellous and strange as this,
        When, bending over me, you do
        Make me forget all else but you.

And now to my blurred eyes come stealing
    Such happy tears, as to confess
Shames no man, from the founts of feeling
    Confused by so much loveliness—
        My blood trembles—my spirit cries
        In wonder, and worships at your eyes!

'Tis passed. A moment—and around me
    Rolls the harsh world again; but love
With one white memory has crowned me—
    Not death itself can rob me of
        That moment, when I saw you there
        Bend down above me through your hair.

BE BORN AGAIN!

VIII

THERE was a time when Love had built apart
 An altar for lone worship in your breast,
 From the world's rage a refuge and a rest,
And drowned her myriad hearts out with one heart.

"Be not as all the others——" all his cry,—
 With terror of oblivion stung, the soul
 Around one loveliest head life's aureole
Flings, 'mid the piteous hosts that hurry by.

But now, to that dear selfhood humbler grown,—
 The woman's heart, so fugitive, frail, and vain—
 Love takes with tears the accustomed lips again,
And the world-arms steal 'round him with your own.

IX

THE long, the autumn rain
    Bows down across the earth,
The flowers die again
    At the breast that gave them birth.

They die at the breast they love,
    They faint and fall away
At the immortal bosom
    In the twilight of the day.

So fain I, too, would die,
    At the last breath to feel
The arms I love the most
    Around my sorrow steal.

O come with silent feet,
    Come where I lie at rest,
Stoop to me with your lips,—
    Cover me with your breast!

And death shall seem familiar,
    Dear, with your heart above,—
So often have I died there,
    So oft, in the hour of love.

X

A PRECIOUS burden did my bosom bear,
    And still in desperation for the one,
That from this breast of dark oblivion
Might rescue it, I hunted everywhere;
With that far lovelier breast of life to share
    The sacred secret that with me alone
    Had perished in the outer night.   But none
Echoed my cry, nor answered to my prayer.

Then through the desert of this life I came
    To the last loneliest marge, and to the sky
Lifted my hands in anguish and in shame,
    And ventured once again the eternal cry,
Calling on the belovèd without name,
    "Where art thou?"   And a voice answered "It is I!"

XI

STORM and black night without—but in this place,
This little lamplit room, what peace I found,
Dear, where the quiet kingdom of your face
Reigns 'mid the lonely terrors ringed around!

XII

SWEET, so insistent, so inexorably
    You cleave and cling to me
Here in this long caress—
Humbling my wayward self to your wild loveliness;
Little you guess,
O dumb, insatiable eagerness,
Little you understand
All that you ask for, all that you demand
Of this worn heart that dies
Here at your own! Sweet life that craves and sighs,
Thirsty beauty and blind—
O loveliness, so tender and so kind,
Compassionate lips and dear,
Can it be you, can it be you that here,
Ceaselessly clamoring,
Demand of love this most extravagant thing
In dread abandonment!
Will you not be content—
Would you have all, all,
Body and heart and spirit for your thrall
Inextricably one—?

BE BORN AGAIN!

Nay, is it not enough that I am none
But yours, yours through and through
Even to the inmost thought
And throne of all my being, is it not
Enough that I am yours, must I be you?

Then, Heart, to be possessed
Recklessly hasten! At that lovelier breast
Give up,—give over!—Take
The death of selfhood, and for beauty's sake
The immortal venture make!
Heart, let us dare.
See—is it not sweet, is it not fair
And worthy of your pain?
Heart—die again—
Die now, and for one shuddering moment live
In the dear being, be
You herself utterly—
So from this breast you shall be born again—:
Heart—give, give!

XIII

LISTEN, dear love, now in this solemn light
  The Eternal Silence speaks. What tremulous,
Sweet, radiant word troubles the moonlit night—
  What is it God is trying to say to us?

XIV

SO royally you dealt with me, so great
　　Your queenly ways of love were! When with me
　You shared your being's bounty, recklessly
I felt your life, triumphant and elate,
Beat at my own that stormed the outer gate;
　　When all my love prayed to you brokenly,
　　With what inexorable ecstasy
Lift to my lips the cup compassionate!

But when deep sleep had summoned you, and when
　　I felt the life that late such largess dealt,
　　　Deep in your breast at battle, play its part
In the lone fight with stealthy death, ah, then
　　Dazed at your side all night I kneeled, and felt
　　　The tragic beating of one human heart.

BE BORN AGAIN!

XV

GREATLY, undauntedly, you did endure
    With brave abandon and supreme consent
  To render up, in the accomplishment
Of life, your holy body and being pure:
Great in surrender, in your giving sure
    And weariless, still with magnificent
    Ardor of love, when love's desire was spent,
Laughed in your eyes the everlasting lure.

And all that loveliness, the loud world's pride,
    Mine in that moment, and how dear I know!
Yet dearer was an hour, when at my side
    You clung with eyes all blinded, and cheeks of snow,—
And beauty broken,—and quivering lips that cried
    Against my lips their piteous human woe.

XVI

THE shoreless and the starless sea of night
    With solemn tide of radiant moonlight flows,
  And gently through the window-lattice throws
Upon your bosom chequered shade and light:
Like a cathedral, bathed in gloom and bright
    With sumptuous splendor, now your body shows—
  In the stern marble of serene repose,
Where reigned the sovereign and supreme delight.

Hushed is your bosom's choir, and deep rest
    Broods on the altar, empty is the throne
And silent is the answer in your breast
    That but so lately echoed to my own—
Where are you fled from me, on what far quest
    In bright disdain, leaving me here alone?

XVII

MUCH had we learned of love, both you and I,
　　His large exuberance and great-hearted days,
　Passionate grief and exquisite delays,
Kinship and mirth beneath the open sky,—
A refuge from the ancient mystery,
　　Love that atones for death in many ways—
　　The love that to the most belovèd prays—
Which is the prayer for immortality.

Yet was the deepest secret still concealed,
　　(Tenderly the great Being uttereth
His truths most awful) till, with eyelids sealed
　　In rapture's dread extreme, and breathless breath,
Your countenance was known; and dawn revealed
　　The face of love which is the face of death.

148

XVIII

THE large days of the everlasting earth
  Draw to sublime conclusion; in the mood
Of ancient autumn, awful and subdued,
She waits the death that is the door to birth—
With bounty bowed against the days of dearth,
  Holy and steadfast—but drear leaves are strewed
  Over the tomb between her breasts, and rude
Wail the huge winds that mock at April's mirth.

Lay your frail arms about my weariness.
  Bare me that pale and patient breast again.
Gather me to you in one deep caress!
  For all my heart is breaking, and the pain
Of life is on me, and the loneliness,—
  And death is dark, and love itself is vain.

XIX

MOONLIGHT is memory; now the sun
His radiant race in heaven has run,
Backward he sheds from far away
The light of our lost yesterday.

On the pillow where your head
Lay dreaming, on the empty bed
Falls the moonlight, on the walls
The lonely light of memory falls.

Where it rested your pale hair
Has left its print in moonlight, where
Your perfect loveliness did press
Lingers a vanished loveliness.

Gaunt in the moonlight the road lies
That took you from my longing eyes,
And one wide window, drenched with light,
Stares out into the marble night. . . .

XX

ACROSS the west the star of evening glides,
　　Toward her, from the under skies that are,
A sister light moves upward in her car,
With the slow pace of beauty that abides.
The face of heaven is breathless like a bride's,
　　But in the solemn vacancies afar
　　Light answers light, star toward belovèd star
In sleepless love through the void heaven rides.

So I to You across the world of things,
　　'Mid shining orbs and vapours uncreate,
　　　　Through the wide waste with changeless motion
　　　　　　climb;
So I to You across the Deep that rings,
　　'Mid glittering wheels and the fixed stars of Fate,
　　　　Answer forever across the womb of Time.

BE BORN AGAIN!

XXI

O YOU, to whom across the universe
    I move along the orbits of my Song,
  Listen to me, and rise above the throng
Of dissonant dischords, the primeval curse!
Not dreams alone are mirrored in this verse,
    But the great truth that makes Creation strong,
    That the heavens ring 'round with like an iron gong,
And the innumerable stars rehearse.

Through harmony, which is necessity
Embraced with love, the very stars are free,
    And hang in heaven thereby, a sacred sign;
And I, through you, shall be caught up above
Myself, and you, beyond yourself, through love
    Console our passion to the laws divine.

*

BE BORN AGAIN!

XXII

I HAVE seen a wondrous vision—stars I have seen,
  Sunset and moonrise—eyes that laugh and weep—
Millions of faces—and the *one* face I have seen:
  The vision falters, and I sleep.

VII

SONG OF THE MOTH

Night into the universe
  Frees us from the walls of day,
And Death, into the starry All,
  When ourselves have passed away.

THE SELF

WHO reigns within my breast, the sovereign lord,
    How many a day this body that he wrought
  On many a dusty road has homeward brought,
Or through the ringing surf that 'round me roared—
Or through my lips the prayer to Beauty poured,
    Or wove the intricate, frail web of thought
    Wherein the flying dream of God is caught—,
Or glowed against the breast of the adored!

How marvellous and strange is he that keeps
    The righteous rather than the evil way,
And in my sleeping bosom never sleeps,
    But holds the ancient enemy at bay;
And comprehends the firmament, and weeps
    Over the fallen dream of yesterday.

WINE OF THE WORLD

CLOSE at the lips of Life I lay
  And drank fresh ardors all the day
From the belovèd eyes and dear
That glowed against me calm and clear.

And reckless still and with unrest
Closer the silent lips I pressed,
But the dark eyes no answer gave,
Burning against me deep and grave.

Day faltered, night drew 'round about,
The heart within me was wearied out;
Then first beyond the dear head I saw
Shadows and swords of the ancient Awe.

And closer I clung, and closer drew
To drink and drain the sweet life through
The lips beloved, but through my fears
Their taste was bitter, as with tears.

WINE OF THE WORLD

O holy draught, and eyes that weep!
Deeper I drank, and deep, and deep:
   The wine of the world is on my lips,
And they are closed in sleep.

ZENITH

NOW in my breast the sole and sovereign Power
     Puts forth his strength, and through a million veins
  I feel the tidal stream of life that strains
Toward the dark sea that doth all streams devour:
This is the noontide of my spirit's hour,
    Through all my frame the imperious rhythm reigns—
    And the one self, that deep in me sustains
His being, stands fulfilled in fullest flower.

Now through my brain the blood's rich purple roars,
    Washing her cells with wine of song and dream,
And in my breast the embattled Splendor wars
    On the dark foe, and rages for extreme
Wrath and delight; and all my being pours
    Through Love and Song toward the escape supreme.

THE PRESENCE

TREMBLING on the utmost brink
  Of thy being, deep I drink:
Swift the opiate moment nears.
I behold thee through my tears.

I behold thy quiet smile,
Bending over me the while,
The dear lips that into mine
Laugh for tenderness divine.

Ah, too deep, ah, fain to pause!
Shuddering, my spirit draws,
Shuddering, I drink and drain
Deep of thee, bewildering pain—

Draught too poignant; in dismay
Fiercely from my lips away
I would press thee, dizzy cup.
Closer thou dost hold it up.

And closer still and closer, dear,
Nearer yet, more near, more near—;

THE PRESENCE

Till I faint of thee, until,
Full of thee, I drink thee still.

Laughing thou dost lift it up
To my lips, that satiate cup:
Thou wouldst have me drink of thee
Deeply, darkly, utterly.

THE MAN TO HIS DEAD POET

IN the small bare room brimmed up with twilight
Hours long in silence I had sat
By the bed on which my youth lay dying
And the poet that I once had been.

Many and many a day he had been failing,
And I knew the end must come at last—
The poor fellow—I had loved him dearly,
It was hard for me to see him go.

He was both my rapture and my sorrow—
O how Love unto its sorrow clings!—
Many a bitter hour had he brought me,
Loneliness, and shipwreck of the heart.

And I loved him. But my mind was weary
Almost as the twilight of the day,
And my soul was sullen, and a little
Tired of his everlasting talk.

Still from side to side his eyes went roaming,
As in fever earnestly he moaned

163

THE MAN TO HIS DEAD POET

Old forgotten ecstasies and splendors,
   Ebbed from out my heart forevermore.

His poor fingers aimlessly and awkward
   Fumbled with the covers, and a look
On his features, fatuous and fervent,
   Foolish seemed and laughable enough.

Softly stirred the curtains. From the river
   Came a sound of whistles. In the street
Flared the first few lamps. A barrel-organ
   Rasped a mournful measure. Night was here.

"Ah, the cities," cried he, "and the faces,
   Like an endless river rolling on—
From what unknown deeps of being risen
   All those myriads, to what shadowy coast

"Of huge doom in sullen grandeur moving,
   The vast waters of the human soul!
Can you see it still—as in an ocean
   Every sea-drop sparkles of the sea,

"Foams, and perishes—, so for a moment
   From each living face the dauntless, dear

THE MAN TO HIS DEAD POET

Eyes of Life look out at us to greet us,
  Shine—and hurry by into the night?

"Is it beautiful," he cried, "my brother?"
  With such fiery question burned his glance,
That to quiet him in haste I answered,
  "All that you have said is doubtless so;

"But, pray, calm yourself, my dear, good fellow,
  Let it be, and let it go at that."
And I drew the covers 'round him closer,
  Smoothed his pillow for him. He began:

"Do you 'mind that night beside the beaches
  When the whole world in one brimming cup,
Earth and sky, the sea, clouds, dews, and starlight,
  To our lips was lifted, and we drank,

"Dizzy with dread joy and sacrificial
  Rapture of self-loss and sorrow dear,
Deep of Beauty's draught, divine nirvana,
  The bewildering wine of all the world?"

"I remember certain lonely beaches,"
  Wearily I answered, "nothing more.

THE MAN TO HIS DEAD POET

Starlight is a usual occurrence
    Any pleasant night beside the sea."

For my heart was sick and sore within me,—
    The poor fellow, every word he spoke
Shamed me, there was something in his gesture
    Almost comic that I could not bear.

Yet I feared this time that I had hurt him
    Such offended silence long he kept:
On his hand I laid my hand in pity,
    Penitent,—and softly he began,

"Ah, that night in May, do you remember?
    Nightingales are singing from the wood—
And the moonlight through the lattice streaming—
    Silence—and deep midnight—and one face,

"Like a moonlit land, desire's kingdom,
    Luring from the breast the homesick self!
Can you see it still" he cried, "my brother?"
    Then in anger broke my wounded heart.

"Streets I see" I said, "and squalid alleys
    Where one lamp flares foully in the night,

THE MAN TO HIS DEAD POET

Darkened windows full of empty faces—
    The sad jest and tragedy of Man!"

"This," he cried aloud, "this, too, is holy—
    O dear Beauty, in what beggar's guise
You may hide your splendor, yet I know you;
    Though the ears be deaf, the eyes be blind,

"Glorious are all things, and forever
    Beautiful and holy is the Real!"
Now I could not answer him, most strangely
    Touched me those old words I knew so well

And I felt the night between us deepen,
    Heard the clock that ticked upon the shelf,
The great silence closing in around us,
    And his hand that he withdrew from mine.

Suddenly he struggled upward laughing,
    Tears of joy were streaming down his face:
In my breast the pang of some departure
    Seized me, and I wept, I know not why.

From a gully of the jaded city
    Drunken laughter filtered through the night

THE MAN TO HIS DEAD POET

Where I knelt, and toward the open window
    Reached my hands before me as in prayer.

"Yes," I whispered it, "this, too, is holy,
    Even this is holy and divine,
Though to poets known and lovers only
    The dear face that looks from meanest things

"And the majesty that moves about us,
    The bright splendor in what common guise.
O dear Beauty, though forever banished,
    Your lost angel by the outer gate,

"Though no more I see, no more may sound it,
    The bright truth that was my very soul;
Let me, baffled still, yet still believing,
    In the darkness loyal to the light,

"Deep within this exiled bosom bear it
    Silent, the great faith forevermore:
Beautiful are all things, and forever
    Holy, holy, holy is the Real!"

From the proud, pale east the patient morning
    Glimmered sadly on a million rooves.

'Round me the old sorrow was awaking,
   And the breaking of some mighty Heart.

On his breast his hands in peace I folded
   Decently, and closed the staring eyes.
He and I had known such days together—
   And I loved him better than myself.

ESCAPE

INTO bright forms the formless Being flows,
  Seeking therein its rapture and repose—
But still the forms subside, and rearise
New forms: body is born and body dies.
Then in my body's cage I murmured, "How
Shall I escape from this destruction now,
This travail all in vain?"
Answered my love, "Escape through love to me
Who am the road to immortality—"
And answered holy Art,
"Build thee a deathless form where thou apart
In lonely immortality shalt reign.
Hasten, and from this fading form depart."

RETURN AFTER DEATH

TO the old home,
 Through the wild country ways and meadows damp,
Lo—I am come:
Drawn are the blinds, quenched is the lonely lamp

And dark the door.
The crickets chirp and the cicadas sing,
But nevermore
Comes the quick step, the dear voice answering.

Long though I knock,
Never the eager answer comes, they will
Never unlock—
So hushed the night, so deep and starry-still.

Ah fain, how fain—
From the dark terror and the loneliness,
Anguish insane
And dreadful secret that you may not guess—

The starry Vast,
Inexorable, of everlasting law,

RETURN AFTER DEATH

Tomb of the Past,
And endless reaches of the ancient Awe,

With horrors rife—
Star upon star forever strewn abroad,
The thrones of life
In the dark universe dethroned of God—

With what desire,
Ah, with what longing that you cannot know!
To the warm fire,
The cosy hearth and faces all aglow,—

Dear eyes that burn,
The old, familiar jokes and questions dear,—
We, lost, return,
Calling with voices that you cannot hear!

Night, deep and still:
Empty into the dark the windows stare—
A whip-poor-will
Cries like the Past upon the patient air—;

But where it lies,
The thing I was, the shell of me, they kneel

RETURN AFTER DEATH

With burning eyes,
And in mute prayer to the Unknown appeal.

Here on the shore
And coast of the illimitable night
Forevermore
Lies the lost shell and home of my delight,

Where passion reigned,
Where ecstasy drew hushed and hurried breath,
Where Love disdained
To stain her triumph with the thought of death.

O pang too sheer
Of all that has been and may never be!
Anguish austere,
And wild regret of all eternity!

THE DEAD POET

NEW mornings flood the world, starred nights wheel
    over;
But he is mute.   Defeated in the war
That virgin Beauty wages on her lover,
    He takes his rest, nor heeds them anymore.

EXILE FROM GOD

I DO not fear to lay my body down
    In death, to share
The life of the dark earth and lose my own,
    If God is there.

I have so loved all sense of Him, sweet might
    Of color and sound,—
His tangible loveliness and living light
    That robes me 'round.

If to His heart in the hushed grave and dim
    We sink more near,
It shall be well—living we rest in Him.
    Only I fear

Lest from my God in lonely death I lapse,
    And the dumb clod
Lose Him; for God is life, and death perhaps
    Exile from God.

VANISHED

HE is not here, your most belovèd one:
　　With everlasting gesture he has cast
　His garments from him, and in splendor passed
Out of the sign and circle of the sun.
He is not with us, he has dared and done
　　The great adventure—, and this frame at last
　Lies, like a shell outworn, here on the vast
Margin and shore of all oblivion.

There is not any motion in the breast
　　Where the quick wave of being came and went—
The bosom thrills not now to be caressed,
　　Nor will the cold lips deign to give consent.
See—he is vanished—and the careless guest
　　Has left his mansion to the element.

THE GREAT SURRENDER

AS at the breast beloved,
    For rapture of sheer excess,
We render up ourselves,
    And are lost in loveliness;

So in a moment supremer,
    More beauty-drunken still,
To the starry choir of All,
    The fires innumerable

Of the universe around us,—
    Radiant, pure and vast,
Faint with immortal rapture,
    To the greater Love at last

Our single, separate selves,
    Freely, beyond recall,
We render up triumphant,
    And sink into the All.

TOWARD THE BRIGHT DOOM

"Darest thou now, O soul—!"

IT was the night when my adventurous soul
Beat at her bars, and toward some ancient goal
Strained through the darkness and emprisoning gloom.
Already 'round me all the little room
Seemed to a vast immensity to spread,
And on the shore and margin of the dread
Kingdom of death, sublime and desolate,
Tiptoe my spirit trembled and elate
With expectation of far things to be.

There was no terror now, no agony;
Only with mute and sorrowful surprise
I felt within my breast the fall and rise
Where the old sovereign still held stubborn sway,
And in my veins the embattled life at bay
Through all the echoing porches of my frame
Reluctantly relinquishing his claim—
The patient pleading of the passionate heart.
And now all this was as a thing apart;
But in the faint night voices, in the breeze

Over the fields, the rustling of the trees,
The owlet's cry that quavered for delight
And poured itself into the poem of night,
A new and an intelligible word
Spoke to my senses, and my spirit heard
In the lone cricket's droning and the shrill
Cicadas' shimmering from vale and hill
The cry of Life, that still in myriad ways
Beseechingly to the belovèd prays,
Seeking therein its immortality—
And Time imploring of Eternity—
The ancient prayer from earth to heaven ascend,
Rapture and ritual without an end,—
And the far surf that broke upon the shore
Broke on my heart in dream forevermore.

Wider and wider did the windows grow,
Toward the soft dark in mute and mournful row
Opening like eyes in everlasting stare,
And wider all the room—till I was 'ware
Of a vague shape that toward the bedside moved
And had the gait and gesture of one loved,—
My mother's, so I dreamed, that now had come
To see me safe abed in the old home,
But more like the belovèd's was the face,

179

And all my being hungered for its grace
Darkly and dumbly: till with sudden awe
Those solemn and those searching eyes I saw,
Kind without pity, patient without scorn,—
O loved and lost before this soul was born!
Out of my breast the very self they stole
That trembled toward that presence, and the whole
Weight of all years, all anguish unexpressed,
I poured out at the patience of that breast,
All griefs, all fears, all hopes uncomforted,
And "O and are you come at last"—I said.

"O take me with you, hasten, let us fly
To the one topmost star of all the sky,
The utmost quivering loveliness afar,
Out of this sorrow of all things that are!
Come—let us haste—let us be fled, and find
Some refuge somewhere surely from this blind
Ruin and wreck of sheer mortality!"
And the roof parted, and in silence we
Through the cool air of quiet evening rose.
I saw the earth beneath me in repose
Glimmering darkly, fields once loved so well,
The little lonely house, and the worn shell
Of my old body on the bed, and one

That knelt beside it with bowed head alone—
Not without grief—ah, not without regret
Was made that mighty sundering! And yet
Over my head the immemorial ways
Of heaven lured me on, the trackless maze
And wilderness of God, sublime and wild;
Then to me turned that face,

"O foolish child,
Where would you seek to? To what loveliness
And dimmest throne of heaven though you press,
What sanctuary of remotest flame,
You shall but find a world of dust, the same
World of old griefs, whither your spirit flow,
But the same world of sorrows left below!
And in what reaches of the farthest Awe
Shall you escape the regnance of the law,
Or on what planet the old face of death,
Or face of love? No light that quivereth
In heaven's holiest in serene disdain
But is a world of passion and of pain
Even as ours, and still the sacred Christ
On every star anew is sacrificed
For the old doom, from age to endless age
Making His everlasting pilgrimage

In lonely splendor down the starry way.
Then whither would you?"

                And I answered, "Nay,
But somewhere surely God has His abode.
Then to that star which is the throne of God,
His very seat, O thither let us first
Stream in fierce love and longing, for I thirst,
Deeply I thirst with deep desire of God!"
And an unbroken silence reigned abroad
Where died those words, where silently was turned
That face toward mine beseeching it, and burned
Deep in those eyes, compassionate and supreme,
Inexorable truth. "Child, child, what dream,
What hopeless hope is here? Where shall you find
This phantom and chimaera of the mind
Reared for your refuge, you, that for your rest,
Have built up God, and given Him a breast
For pain to lean on, and a heart for love!
Though from heaven's deeps to heaven's heights above
You seek Him, though through all eternity
You send your soul out in one loneliest cry,
No voice shall answer, nor no tongue declare
The Presence that is all things everywhere—
The flying Dream." Then on my spirit fell

That bolt of truth like lightning terrible,—
Nor might I speak, nor might I think, that felt
Out of my soul that thought supremest melt,
That hope the dearest; but from all heaven there waned
Some Light that through the universe had reigned
In holiest beauty: and I whispered low,
"Even as you will, do with me even so."

Midway in heaven we paused, was lifted up
Now to my faltering lips a drowsy cup
Upon whose cold, clear brim, as on the brink
Of nothingness, shuddered my lips, and "Drink"
Cried a low voice, "deep of this draught divine,—
Oblivion, the world's consoling wine—
Wine of all tears and sorrows and dark sleep,
Nirvana, great and blessed—deep, deep
Drink, and in holy love triumphantly
Render your self up to the All, and be
In other selves your immortality!
Amen. Amen." What mastery forsook
This soul, unkingdomed then! What terror shook
This throne of being to its shrillest cry,
"This weary self, this bitter self, this I,
This weak and foolish, this inglorious one,
This self, *this* self, and not oblivion,

TOWARD THE BRIGHT DOOM

This only, *this* forever, *this* alone,
This and no other—!" So my being's wave
Broke on fate's shore in agony.

                    But grave
Were the calm eyes that searched me, and austere
The awful voice that answered, "Shall you fear
To render up what all have loved and lost?
Would you through timeless Time, a lonely ghost,
In solitary selfishness apart
Wander the heavens, from the eternal heart
Of Life an exile? Shall you dread to move
Into the blood and breast of all you love
In gracious self-surrender, shrink to take
The cup, supreme and bitter, for the sake
Of all dear life, nor generously give
Your self up in the self of all that live—
This broken and bruised spirit bravely yield
To be ploughed under, furrowed and rent, a field
Harrowed and cleft, in glorious martyrdom,
For holier harvests on far days to come,
Beings more lovely in some worthier shape?
Nay, would you the one common doom escape
Of all those silent millions that did bear
Their part in death and suffered it, nor share

TOWARD THE BRIGHT DOOM

The general lot of all men born to be,
And the great sacrament universal? See,
On all these myriad thrones of Life there shall
No life escape the destiny tragical
And doom triumphant! See, the summer's rose,
That to the sunlight did herself unclose,
Gently into the dust her head inclines—
The swallow fleet, that in sweet heaven shines
A flickering flame, ceaselessly hurries by
Into the great repose, nor questions why
In its brief heart, and in the ringing wood
All songs most musical are soon subdued
To the great peace; while all things gay and dear,
Springtime and April of the flowering year,
In generous self-abandonment consent
To the sublime and dark accomplishment
Of life's divine renewals: Loveliness
On death's divide in a supreme caress
Shatters her beauty, like a moonlit wave!
Yea, the one body dear and bounty brave,
The lips of life, full of all sweet replies,
That had the breath of Springtime in their sighs,
That held the immortal boon, the very breast,
Framed for all joys and born to be caressed,
In stately splendor through the gathering gloom

185

TOWARD THE BRIGHT DOOM

Moves without murmur, and accepts the doom—
Yea, even this, the most belovèd, too!
Now in this thought perish the thought of you,
And in the wonder and the dream thereof
Cease, and be one at last with all you love."

Then toward those eyes, pleading I turned, and saw
Pity inexorable, eternal awe.
And on the starry All that 'round me moved
I looked, and on the universe I loved.
And to the dregs that cup of hopes and fears
I drained with fiery laughter and wild tears!

HOLY LIGHT

LIFE, where your lone candle burns
    In the darkness of the night,
Mothlike my lost spirit yearns
    Nearer in its circling flight.

Luringly your beauty draws
    Onward with each shuddering breath,
Till I flutter,—till I pause
    In the radiance of death.

I am flaming, I am fled—
    All around you reigns the night;
But my agony has fed
    You a moment, holy light!